Dear Parent:
Your child's love of reading starts here!

Every child learns to read in a different way and at his or her own speed. You can help your young reader improve and become more confident by encouraging his or her own interests and abilities. You can also guide your child's spiritual development by reading stories with biblical values and Bible stories, like I Can Read! books published by Zonderkidz. From books your child reads with you to the first books he or she reads alone, there are I Can Read! books for every stage of reading:

 SHARED READING
Basic language, word repetition, and whimsical illustrations, ideal for sharing with your emergent reader.

 BEGINNING READING
Short sentences, familiar words, and simple concepts for children eager to read on their own.

 READING WITH HELP
Engaging stories, longer sentences, and language play for developing readers.

 READING ALONE
Complex plots, challenging vocabulary, and high-interest topics for the independent reader.

 ADVANCED READING
Short paragraphs, chapters, and exciting themes for the perfect bridge to chapter books.

Can Read! books have introduced children to the joy of reading since 1957. Featuring award-winning authors and illustrators and a fabulous cast of beloved characters, I Can Read! books set the standard for beginning readers.

A lifetime of discovery begins with the magical words **"I Can Read!"**

Visit www.icanread.com for information on enriching your child's reading experience.
Visit www.zonderkidz.com for more Zonderkidz I Can Read! titles.

Man looks at how someone appears on the outside.
But I [God] look at what is in the heart.
—*1 Samuel 16:7*

To my great nieces—
Brittany, Ashlynn, Leeanna, and Emma.
~M.H.

The Princess Twins Play in the Garden
Text copyright © 2009 by Mona Hodgson
Illustrations copyright © 2009 by Meredith Johnson

Requests for information should be addressed to:
Zonderkidz, Grand Rapids, Michigan 49530

Library of Congress Cataloging-in-Publication Data

Hodgson, Mona Gansberg, 1954-
    The princess twins play in the garden / story by Mona Hodgson ; pictures by Meredith Johnson.
        p. cm. -- (I can read! Level 1)
    ISBN 978-0-310-71608-2 (softcover)
    [1. Princesses--Fiction. 2. Christian life--Fiction.] I. Johnson, Meredith, ill. II. Title.
    PZ7.H6649Pv 2009
    [E]--dc22
                                                            2008037324

Art Direction & Design: Jody Langley

Printed in China

09 10 11 12 • 4 3 2 1

ZONDERkidz | I Can Read!™ | BEGINNING READING 1

The Princess Twins Play in the Garden

story by Mona Hodgson

pictures by Meredith Johnson

Princess Emma and Princess Abby
walked in the castle garden.

"God made this a lovely day,"

Princess Abby said to her sister.

Emma stopped and screamed.

"There's a bug on my pretty dress."

"It will get my dress dirty.

Get it off of me!" Emma said.

Abby gently lifted the ladybug

and set it on a rose.

"Thank you," Emma said.

Abby and Emma saw their friends.

"It's time for our play date,"

said Abby.

Princess Abby ran down the hill.

Princess Emma walked down the hill.

She didn't want her dress

to get dirty.

She wanted to look pretty.

Mrs. Lee said good-bye
to her children.
"Have fun at the castle,"
said Mrs. Lee.

"Let's play in the garden,"
said Princess Abby.
The children ran up the hill
to the castle.

"We can have tea," said Emma.

"I don't want to get dirty."

The children had a tea party
in the garden.

Abby gave her friends rides
on her pony.

Emma sat in a chair and watched.

"A princess must look pretty,"
Emma said.

Abby and her friends
made sand castles.

The children played soccer
with Princess Abby.

A muddy ball hit Emma's dress.

"How could you?" she said

to the little girl who'd kicked it.

The little girl stared at Emma.

"I'm sorry," she said.

Tears filled the girl's eyes.

Emma was sorry she'd yelled.

"That's okay," she said.

Emma hugged the little girl.

"Let's play," said Emma.

She kicked the soccer ball.

It was time to go home.

Mrs. Lee waved.

Emma and Abby ran down the hill
with the children.

"Mama, we had lots of fun,"

said the children.

Mrs. Lee smiled at the princesses.

"Thank you," she said.

"You are both lovely girls."

A ladybug landed on Emma's dress.

She smiled and prayed,

"Thank you, God, for a lovely day."